Introduction to Ecology and Environmental Laws in India

By Siva Prasad Bose

Published by Joy Bose

Copyright © 2022 Siva Prasad Bose and Joy Bose

All Rights Reserved

Contents

Dedication

Preface

Acknowledgements

Chapter 1: Introduction to Ecology

Chapter 2: Introduction to Environment and Environmental Protection

Chapter 3: List of Environmental Laws in India

Chapter 4: Environment Protection in the Indian Constitution

Chapter 5: Forest Conservation Act 1980

Chapter 6: Water Act 1974

Chapter 7: Air Act 1981

Chapter 8: Environment Protection Act 1986

Chapter 9: Coastal Regulation Zone Notification 2018

Chapter 10: Hazardous Waste Management Regulations

Chapter 11: Energy Conservation Act 2001

Chapter 12: Scheduled Tribes and Other Traditional Forest Dwellers (Recognition of Forest Rights) Act, 2006 (FRA)

Chapter 13: Biological Diversity Act 2002

Chapter 14: National Green Tribunal Act (NGT) 2010

Chapter 15: Wildlife Protection Act 1972

Chapter 16: Conclusion

About the author

Other books by Siva Prasad Bose

Dedication

This book is dedicated to all the Indian environment, environmental activists in India and all people who are affected by environmental pollution in India.

Preface

The environment is one of the most precious resources that is available to any country and its people. For rapidly developing countries like India, there are a range of environmental problems such as pollution, deforestation, disappearance of wildlife and sea life. Environmental laws are thus needed to protect and preserve the environment from destruction.

In this book, we first present an introduction to issues related to ecology and environment. We then summarize the main laws that are available to protect the environment. These laws cover different aspects of the environment such as wildlife, pollution control, forest cover and waste management. Taken together, these laws present a comprehensive system to protect and preserve the biodiversity and environmental resources connected with the air, water and soil of India.

It is hoped that this book would provide a good introductory guidance to people who are interested in environmental issues and who wish to be familiar with the laws in India related to the environment.

Acknowledgements

In writing this book, the authors gratefully acknowledge help from the following sources of information:

- McGraw-Hill Concise Encyclopaedia of Science and Technology. Sybil P Parker (Editor), McGraw Hill, 1984
- The Ecology Book: Big Ideas Simply Explained. Dorling Kindersley, 2019

Chapter 1: Introduction to Ecology

In this chapter we introduce some introductory concepts of ecology and its aspects related to the environment.

1.1 What is Ecology

Ecology is the study of the relation of organisms to their environment. It is concerned with the biology of groups of organisms and with functional processes in the lands, oceans, rivers and lakes. It is the study of the structure and function of nature. It can be considered as part of biology and its taxonomic divisions, which are concerned with fundamentals common to all life, as well as with unifying principles applicable to nature as a whole. Ecology may also include the environmental relations of individuals or species, as well as communities of organisms.

Ecology is a vast subject embracing many disciplines to understand the relationships between living species and the physical ecosystems where they live. It includes the knowledge gained from different branches of science such as biology, zoology, chemistry and physics, as well as aspects of social science such as economics, while raising profound philosophical and ethics questions.

Since we humans depend on natural systems, ecology also influences some important political issues such as climate change, ozone layer, rising sea levels, disappearance of wildlife or sea-life and extraction of fossil fuels.

1.2 Approaches to Ecology

Ways in which one may subdivide ecology include the following:

- One way to subdivide ecology is in terms of **level of organization** beyond the level of individual organisms. The levels may be divided into, protoplasm, cells, tissues, organs, organ systems, organisms, populations, communities and ecosystems.

- Another way is to divide ecology on the basis of **organisms or taxonomic groups** of organisms studied, such as insect ecology.

- Another way is based on the **kind of habitat or environment** to be studied, such as marine ecology, freshwater ecology and so on.

In ecology the term of population, originally used to denote a group of people, is broadened to include groups of individuals of any one species of organism. Community in the ecological sense, sometimes designated as a biotic community, includes all the species population of a given situation.

The community or individual and the non-living environment function together as an ecological system or **ecosystem**.

The earth as an ecosystem is commonly terms as the **biosphere**.

It should be noted that some of the attributes of organisms may be common or integrated as a result of some checks and balances and forces of nature. For example, the rate of photosynthesis of a whole forest or a field may be more common than that of the individual plants, since when one individual in the species slows down, others may speed up to compensate.

1.3 Subdivisions of Ecology

Some types of ecology include the following:

- **System ecology**: Exploring quantitative and qualitative relations with the help of mathematical concepts.

- **Synecology**: Study of groups of organisms such as communities.

- **Autecology**: Study of environmental relations of individuals or species.

- **Applied ecology**: This involves the application of ecological principles and knowledge of principles and techniques of ecosystems to solve human problems such as specific environmental problems and management of the biosphere as an integral whole. Humans are an integral part of the ecosystem and depend on its healthy functioning for their continued well-being.

Figure: Ecosystem. AI generated art by Midjourney AI

1.4 Ecosystem

Ecosystem, short for ecological system, refers to a functioning system that includes the organisms of a community together with their environment. It includes all natural communities or assemblages of organisms which live together and interact with one another and are closely related to their environment.

The term 'ecosystem' can be applied to any size or level of environment that is chosen to be studied, such as micro communities within a decaying log or bigger scale communities such as a forest. Even all the organisms of the world may be considered as a world community forming a single world ecosystem, whose living part is the biosphere.

The following aspects of organisms in relation to their ecosystem can be identified:

- Its **location**, described in terms of physical and chemical factors.
- The kind of community, constituting its **functional habitat**.
- Its place within the community including its relationship with other organisms.

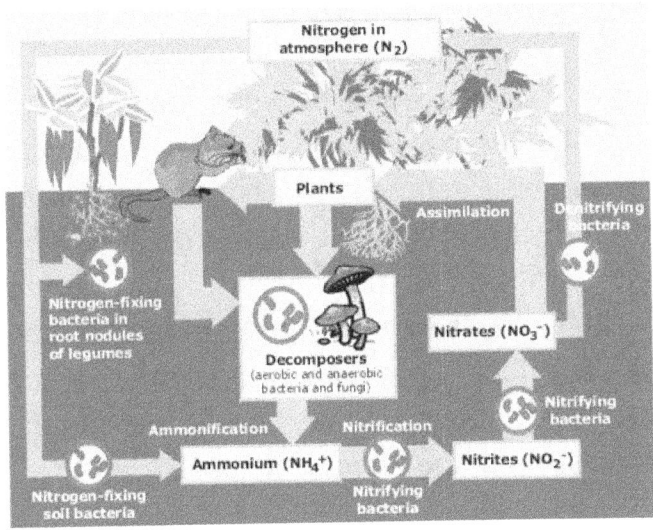

Figure: Nitrogen cycling in an ecosystem. U.S. Environmental Protection Agency, Public domain, via Wikimedia Commons

Within an ecosystem, certain major fractions or divisions may be identified. For example, a terrestrial ecosystem may have 4-5 subdivisions as follows:

- The physical environment, such as climate.
- The soil, if distinguished from physical environment
- The vegetation or plant community.
- The animal community.
- The saprobe community comprising bacteria and fungi.

1.5 Ecological Interactions

This refers to the relationships between members of different species belonging to a particular ecological community. Ecologists generally classify interactions according to the effect on the population growth rate by members of one species on another species. If increase in one results in the increase of the growth rate of the second species, the effect is positive, else negative. If the first species results in neither increase nor decrease in the growth rate of the second, the effect is neutral.

The effect on growth rate may be direct or indirect. A direct effect can be, for example, due to territorial fighting between members of different species. An indirect effect may be by involving a third species. For example, earthworms increase plant growth and thus provide more food for caterpillars, increasing their growth rate as well.

Interspecies competition occurs when two species negatively affect one another. The main kinds of such competition are as follows:

- **Exploitation competition** between species: This occurs when individuals of one species deprive another by consuming a resource such as food, reducing their population growth rate.

- **Interference competition**: This occurs when members of a species directly harm another, such as by producing toxins, killing, fighting or injuring them.

- **Subtle types of competition**: These may occur when individuals from different species interact in a way so as to use energy that might have been used otherwise for the production of offspring, thus harming the growth rate.

- **Predation**: This occurs when individuals of one species (predator) consume another (prey). In this interaction the predator benefits and the prey are harmed. Either predator or prey, or both, can be an animal, plant or parasite. Examples can be a hawk eating a sparrow, a sparrow eating a seed, venus flytrap eating an insect, a tick drawing blood from a dog, or a bacteria that infects a human.

- **Mutualism**: This occurs when two species positively affect one another. This interaction may be essential for survival of one or both species, or non-essential (called protocooperation). For example, termites that consume wooden plant parts are dependent on protozoa in their guts to digest cellulose. Some plants depend on bacteria which extract nitrogen from airspaces in the soil and make it available to the plant. Lichens are composed of algae and fungi, where the algae can photosynthesize and provide various organic compounds to fungi, and fungi can dissolve nutrients from the rock on which algae live.

- **Commensalism**: This occurs when one species positively affects another but is itself little affected. Examples include plants such as orchids that grow on other plants such as trees: the former is benefited, and the latter is not affected much.

1.6 Ecological Succession

This refers to a gradual process brought about by the change in the number of individuals of each species of a community by the establishment of new species populations which may gradually replace the original inhabitants.

Such succession can depend on several factors:

- Flora and fauna of the region in general i.e., which organisms are in a position to invade a site.
- The rate of change of the habitat and its receptivity to the potential invaders.
- Chance factors which may influence interactions

The term sere is used to describe all the temporary communities which occur during a successional sequence in a given site. Eventually succession ends, and changes in the species composition of the community either ceases or fluctuates within some bounds.

Succession sequences may be classified on the basis of starting habitat. Some examples are as follows:

- **Hydroseres** are communities in which pioneering plants invade open water, eventually forming some kind of soil such as peat or muck.
- **Xeroseres** are communities on dry and sterile ground such as rock, sand or clay.

If an open habitat has never been occupied before, the way is opened for primary succession. If the habitat has been disturbed, leaving vestiges of soil, seeds or other organic debris from the previous occupancy, a secondary succession will begin.

As an area is invaded and taken over by successive populations of plants and animals, the character and composition of the community changes. Isolated pioneer plants eventually give way to a consolidation of the plant cover. New species which can better utilize the resources of the habitat gradually take over. Finally, the climax community is established, and can perpetuate stably over time since the birth rate is stable.

An understanding of succession is important for effective human management of communities. Human activities generally have the effect of controlling or stopping succession in the following ways:

- Fire can be used to keep forests suitable for hunting or agriculture, by clearing away the underbrush.

- Since most major crop plants are annuals of the pioneer stage, regular ploughing is needed to hold down succession.

- Through mowing and grazing, which favour grasses and kill tree seedlings

- By selective weed control with herbicide chemicals.

- Succession can be either retarded or accelerated by manipulation of drainage. This may be used, for example, to establish a protective timber. A forest must be managed to allow the species of trees to grow free from competition.

1.7 Predator Prey Equations

Ecological processes such as the relation between predator and prey populations can be modelled using mathematical equations called Lotka–Volterra equations. These are first order nonlinear differential equations to model the dynamics of the populations. An example is the predator prey relationship between herbivores such as deer and carnivores such as tigers or lions.

Figure: Tiger hunting a deer. AI generated art by DALL-E 2 AI art generator.

These equations assume the following:

- The prey typically has limitless access to food and its population grows, however when they meet a predator they are eaten.

- The predator population will grow only if they have more prey to eat, however if the predators are unable to catch their prey or if there are too many predators and too few prey, they will die out.

- Rate of change of population is proportional to its size

- The evolutionary pressure on the prey is to escape from the predator and survive to have more offspring, while the predator has to catch more prey to provide food for more offspring.

- The appetite of predators is limitless

This leads to a never-ending struggle between the predator and prey varying from near extinction to growth of the population.

Hence the population change across time can be modelled by the following Lotka–Volterra equations:

$dx/dt = \alpha x - \beta xy$

$dy/dt = \delta xy - \gamma y$

where

- x is the number of prey such as deer
- y is the number of some predator such as lions
- dx/dt and dy/dt represent the instantaneous growth rates of the two populations;
- t represents time;
- $\alpha, \beta, \gamma, \delta$ are positive real parameters describing the interaction of the two species.

The solution of the equation modelling the population of the predator prey species is given as follows:

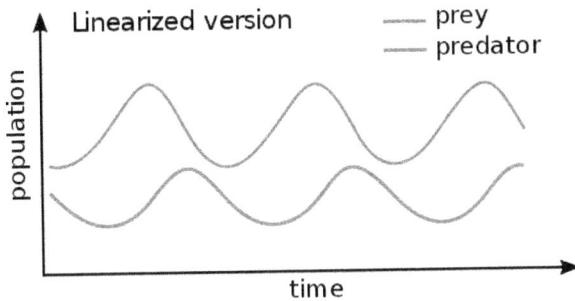

Figure: Result of the predator prey equations modelling the populations of predator and prey species across time. AspidistraK, CC BY-SA 4.0 via Wikimedia Commons

While the predator prey equations offer an insight into the population dynamics of two species, the assumptions may not be reflected in real-life and it may be more complex and other factors in the ecosystem also effect their populations.

1.8 Ecological Niche

The concept of ecological niche is another important concept in ecology. An organism's niche includes how it fits within the environment, the environmental factors and relationships of the organism with the community and ecosystem, including the combination of its place and role in the environment. It includes how the organism meets its needs for food and shelter, how it avoids predators, competes with other species and reproduces. The niche also includes the organism's interactions with other organisms, such as predation and competition and the non-living environment and environmental conditions.

A unique niche is an advantage for any animal or plant because this reduces competition with other species and enables the species to adapt successfully and survive with a better growth rate. For ecologists, a full knowledge of an organism's niche is vital to form interventions to compensate for environmental changes such as habitat destruction and climate change which threaten the organism's survival.

Ecological niches depend on the existence of a stable habitat, which is the place where the organism lives. Small changes in habitat can influence or destroy the niches that the organism used to fill.

For example, the species known as dragonfly have the following niche:

- The larvae develop in a certain range of water acidity, chemical composition, temperature and prey, and with a limited number of predators.

- The right vegetation is needed by adult females for egg laying and by larva for metamorphosis.

- The dragonfly also impacts its environment: its eggs are food for amphibians, its larvae which are both predators and prey add nutrients to the water, and the adults prey on insects.

These requirements and impacts define its ecological niche. For a species to persist, conditions have to be within the required ranges, else it could face extinction.

1.9 The Principle of Competition between Organisms

Competition is the driver of evolution of species. The need to be bigger, stronger and better leads to adaptations by the species that provides them an edge in survival compared to other species. When two species compete for identical resources, the one with advantages will outdo the weaker one, which will either adapt so it no longer competes and finds its unique ecological niche, or else become extinct. However, both the competing populations cannot coexist at constant population values. This proposition is known as the **competitive exclusion principle** and was first proposed by Russian microbiologist Gregory Gause and thus known as Gause's law.

There are two main types of competition as per Gause's law

- **Intraspecific competition**: competition between members of the same species. This ensures that only the healthiest or best adapted individuals within the same species can survive.

- **Interspecific competition**: This is competition between different species that reply on the same resources. Here too, the most well adapted species will survive.

Competition may be direct or indirect. There are the following two modes of competition:

- **Exploitation**: The organisms interact indirectly, by both consuming the common resource they depend on, where less is left for the others.

- **Interference**: Here the organisms directly compete for the same resource.

Chapter 2: Introduction to Environment and Environmental Protection

In this chapter we introduce some aspects of the biotic and abiotic environment, as well as methods and legislation to protect the environment in various countries.

2.1 Biotic and Abiotic Environment

Environment is the sum of all external conditions and influences effecting the life and development of organisms.

Two main aspects of the environment are the following:

- **Biotic**: This includes the organisms living in the environment.
- **Abiotic**: This includes the non-living (physical and chemical) aspects of the environment.

2.2 Abiotic environment

The physical or abiotic environment includes the non-living aspects that influence living organisms. Such factors include soil, water, temperature, atmosphere and energy from various sources.

One of the main forms of energy that influences organisms is radiant energy received from the sun, as well as infrared radiation or heat, visible radiation and ionising radiation. These energies are subject to modifying factors and seasonal cycles and influenced by atmospheric conditions, latitude, altitude, slope, exposure, cover etc.

The intensity aspect of heat energy is temperature. Along with moisture and light, it is the most familiar aspect of the environmental conditions. Except for birds and mammals, the body temperature of plant and animal life is determined primarily by the external environment.

Light of the sun and moon are the primary sources with sufficient intensity to support life. Light is used for photosynthesis by plants, as well as used for vision in animals, and also effects growth and survival.

Water and air are fundamental media on which life exists. They provide the basis for the division of the world into aquatic and terrestrial environments. Water covers 70% of the earth's surface and also provides for survival of life within the depths of rivers, seas and oceans.

The atmosphere contains the gases nitrogen, oxygen, carbon dioxide, other gases in smaller quantities as well as water vapour. Oxygen and carbon dioxide effect all forms of life through photosynthesis and respiration, through their reciprocal relationship of synthesis and decomposition.

2.3 Biotic environment

The biotic environment consists of living organisms which interact with each other and are also interrelated with their abiotic environment.

The interactions can be divided as follows:

- **Within a population of the same species**: Interactions between organisms include aspects such as density, birth rate, death rate, age distribution, dispersion and growth forms.

- **Between different species**: At the inter species population level, the interactions include competition, predation, parasitism, commensalism, cooperation and mutualism.

- **At the community level**: Interactions include dominance and succession. In dominance, one or several species control the habitat. In succession, there is an orderly process of community change. Rhythmic change in community is termed periodicity.

- **Interactions with abiotic environment**: These include the effects of organisms on the microenvironment through temperature, water, wind and light. They also include the modification of substrata through soil building. Finally, they include the modification of the medium, as in aquatic habitats.

2.4 Environmental Engineering

Environmental engineering is the discipline that evaluates the effect of humans on the environment and develops controls to minimize degradation of the environment.

In recent times, governments have become aware of the deterioration of air, water and land through human activity as part of economic development. The roots of the problem lies in the rapid growth of the national population as well as the industrial development of national resources. Hence, legislation in various countries has focused on the preservation of these resources.

The ultimate goal of environmental engineering is the design of processes and systems that need minimal treatment for pollution control and recycling of wastes for reuse. Government policy in different countries is aimed at achieving this goal. The United Nations (UN) also makes similar goals and targets to encourage other countries to meet their environmental sustainability goals.

Figure: Sewage dumped into a river. AI generated art by Midjourney AI

2.5 Environmental Protection

Environmental protection refers to the steps taken that limit harm to the quality of water, air and land used by humans. It includes **conservation**, which is to care for and protect the earth's natural resources including air, water, soil, minerals, plants and animals so as to benefit all living beings including humans. Human activities produce wastes that are vapours or gases, solids, liquids or energy states, which are dispersed to the open environment of water, air or land and affect all forms of life. Environmental protections include limiting the harm from such activities.

Environmental protection has the following objectives:

- Protect people from physiological damage from pathogenic organisms, toxic chemicals and from excess of physical energies.

- Protect humans from irritation and discomfort from unfavourable conditions in water, air or land.

- Safeguard the balance in the earth's ecosystems and conserve natural resources.

2.6 Pollution and Control of Pollutants

When human-generated waste released into water, air and land overwhelms the natural process of assimilation of such wastes, **pollution** occurs. Large urban and industrial areas with the massive use of internal combustion engines in cars etc. for transportation increase air pollution, since the airborne waste loads exceed the capacity of horizontal and vertical air movements to disperse the materials. Similarly, industrial effluents and wastes from cities are spilled into rivers thereby polluting them. Same is the issue of dumping wastes in landfills. Also, conditions of inversion, stagnation and ultraviolet radiation produce reactants from primary pollutants. On land and water, not all wastes are usable as food for natural biota and are thus labelled non-biodegradable. Similarly, chlorinated hydrocarbon pesticides are high on the list of persistent contaminants which pollute the environment.

The solutions to control the pollution of the environment from the wastes are as follows:

- Eliminate the source of pollution
- Eliminate the wastes that are dumped on the sea, land and air
- Treat the waste to reduce the pollution
- Augment the environmental capacity to assimilate the wastes.

For wastewater, the solution is to promote natural processes through which carbohydrates, proteins and fats in the wastewater are consumed by bacteria in the presence of sufficient oxygen. The settled solids or sludge are separated and made the food of anaerobic organisms in sludge digestors. Similar techniques can be used to remove particulates from the airstream.

2.7 Environmental laws in the US (to compare with India)

In this section, we briefly look at some of the environmental laws made by the United States government, since US is not only one of the most powerful nations but also has been one of the most polluting ones. The laws in India, Europe and other countries are also broadly similar and comparable.

The federal government in the US, as well as the governments of different US states, have both enacted environmental legislation concerning air, water and land use. The main laws at the US federal level include the following:

- Wilderness act of 1964
- Air quality act of 1967, followed by the clean air act of 1970 and its subsequent amendments
- Water quality act of 1965, replaced by the water pollution control act of 1972
- National environment policy act of 1969
- Noise control act and coastal zone management act of 1972
- Resource conservation and recovery act of 1976
- Surface mining control and reclamation act of 1977 and toxic substances control act of 1977

These have been followed by corresponding acts at the state level as well.

The national environmental policy act, for example, mandates an in-depth study of environmental impact with any new industrial or government activity that involves the government.

Another important environmental move in the US was the formation of the Environmental Protection Agency or EPA in 1970, which has the responsibility of setting standards and a compliance timetable for air and water quality improvement, along with administering the noise control act, resource conservation and recovery act, toxic substances control act and so on. The agency also administers grants to state and local governments on construction of wastewater treatment facilities and for air and water pollution control.

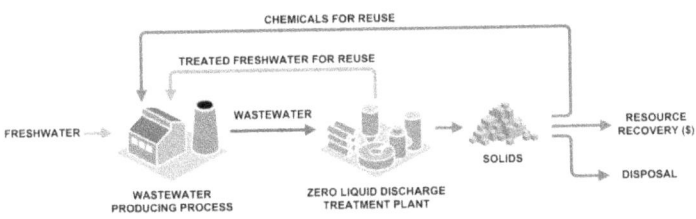

Figure: Wastewater treatment process in a sewage treatment plant. Saltworks Technologies, CC BY-SA 4.0 <https://creativecommons.org/licenses/by-sa/4.0>, via Wikimedia Commons

Along with laws for environmental protection, the industrial policy also plays a role. For example, industries that extract natural resources from the earth, thus disturbing the surface, are being called to restore the land to a state that is similar or better than the original state.

The Surface Mining Coal and Reclamation Act, which covers coal mining, requires states to have an EPA approved program to reclaim abandoned mining lands and control surface mining operations. Similarly, liquid wastes can be treated by chemical or physical means or a combination of them to remove most of the contaminants and recycle the liquid. Air or gaseous contaminants can be removed by scrubbing, filtration, absorption or adsorption and the clean gas discharged into the atmosphere. The removed contaminants, either dry or in solution, must be handled wisely, or else they can lead to new pollution related problems.

Chapter 3: List of Environmental Laws in India

In this chapter we list some important laws in India that are vital for protection and conservation of the environment.

The main laws in India for environmental protection include the following:

- Acts related to water
    - Water (Prevention and Control of Pollution) Act 1974 (Water Act).
- Acts related to air
    - Air (Prevention and Control of Pollution) Act 1981 (Air Act).
- Acts related to the general environment
    - Environment (Protection) Act 1986 (EP Act).
- Acts related to waste management
    - E-Waste (Management) Rules 2016 (E-Waste Rules)

- Batteries (Management & Handling) Rules 2001
- Bio-Medical Waste Management Rules 2016
- Plastic Waste Management Rules 2016
- Solid Waste Management Rules 2016
- Construction and Demolition Waste Management Rules 2016
- Hazardous and Other Waste (Management and Transboundary Movement) Rules 2016
- Manufacture, Storage and Import of Hazardous Chemicals Rules 1989 (MSIHC Rules);

- Acts related to protection of coastal zones
  - Coastal Regulation Zone Notification 2019
  - Environment Impact Assessment Notification 2006.

- Acts related to preservation of wildlife and conservation of forests and biodiversity
  - Wildlife (Protection) Act 1972.
  - Forest (Conservation) Act 1980.

- - Scheduled Tribes and Other Traditional Forest Dwellers (Recognition of Forest Rights) Act 2006 (FRA)
  - Biological Diversity Act 2002.
- Act to set up the National green tribunal
  - National Green Tribunal Act 2010.
- Public Liability Insurance Act 1991

In the following chapters, we shall study some of these acts in more detail.

Chapter 4: Environment Protection in the Indian Constitution

In this chapter we discuss the environmental protections granted in the Indian constitution. The protections are mainly mentioned under the directive principles of state policy and the fundamental duties.

4.1 Article 21 of the constitution

The Article 21 in The Constitution of India states the following:

Protection of life and personal liberty

No person shall be deprived of his life or personal liberty except according to procedure established by law

This article has also been interpreted as the right of citizens to a clean and healthy environment.

4.2 Environmental Protection in the Directive Principles of State Policy (Part IV) Article 48A

The directive principles of state policy in the constitution of India state the following:

Protection and improvement of environment and safeguarding of forests and wildlife The State shall endeavour to protect and improve the environment and to safeguard the forests and wildlife of the country.

4.3 Fundamental duties (Part IV A) Article 51A

The fundamental duties mentioned in the Indian Constitution state the following:

To protect and improve the natural environment including forests, lakes, rivers, and wildlife, and to have compassion for living creatures.

4.4 Conclusion

In this chapter we have gone through the wildlife protection related clauses in the Indian constitution. While these mainly come under fundamental duties and under directive principles of state policy, their inclusion in the constitution shows how seriously the framers valued the preservation and protection of wildlife.

Chapter 5: Forest Conservation Act 1980

In this chapter we discuss the Forest Conservation Act 1980. This act is intended to ensure the conservation of India's forests and the resources of the forests.

> THE FOREST (CONSERVATION) ACT, 1980
> ACT No. 69 OF 1980
>
> [27th December, 1980.]
>
> An Act to provide for the conservation of forests and for matters connected therewith or ancillary or incidental thereto.
>
> BE it enacted by Parliament in the Thirty-first Year of the Republic of India as follows:—
>
> **1. Short title, extent and commencement.**—(*1*) This Act may be called the Forest (Conservation) Act, 1980.
>
> (*2*) It extends to the whole of India except the State of Jammu and Kashmir.
>
> (*3*) It shall be deemed to have come into force on the 25th day of October, 1980.
>
> **2. Restriction on the dereservation of forests or use of forest land for non-forest purpose.**—Notwithstanding anything contained in any other law for the time being in force in a State, no State Government or other authority shall make, except with the prior approval of the Central Government, any order directing—
>
> (*i*) that any reserved forest (within the meaning of the expression "reserved forest" in any law for the time being in force in that State) or any portion thereof, shall cease to be reserved;
>
> (*ii*) that any forest land or any portion thereof may be used for any non-forest purpose.
>
> *Explanation.*—For the purposes of this section "non-forest purpose" means the breaking up or clearing of any forest land or portion thereof for any purpose other than reafforestation.
>
> **3. Constitution of Advisory Committee.**—The Central Government may constitute a Committee consisting of such number of persons as it may deem fit to advise that Government with regard to—
>
> (*i*) the grant of approval under section 2; and

Figure: First page of the Forest Conservation Act 1980

5.1 Forest Conservation Act 1980

Forests are a unique natural resource and support a variety of animal and plant life. Due to rapid industrialization and also encroaching of forest land for agriculture and grazing purposes, parts of India's forest land were in danger of deforestation. Hence to preserve the forest cover and to protect the forests from getting cleared, the Forest Conservation Act was brought.

This is a rather short act. It mainly restricts the use of reserved forest land for any other purpose, such as by clearing up the forest land. It restricts the de-reserving of reserved forest land, without prior approval of the central government. It constitutes an advisory committee by the central government for purposes of forest conservation. It also declares penalties for contravening the provisions of the act. The power to make rules under this act lies with the central government alone.

5.2 Forest (Conservation) Amendment Act 2023

In August 2023, the Indian Parliament passed the Forest (Conservation) Amendment Act 2023, which came into force on August 4, 2023, and introduced significant changes to the Forest Conservation Act 1980. The amended Act was also renamed in Hindi as the Van (Sanrakshan Evam Samvardhan) Adhiniyam, 1980. This amendment is among the most significant changes to India's forest protection framework in decades and has generated considerable debate among conservationists, legal experts, and tribal communities.

The key changes introduced by the 2023 amendment are as follows:

Clarification of the Act's scope: The original 1980 Act was interpreted broadly to cover all land that fulfilled the dictionary meaning of "forest" following a landmark Supreme Court judgment in the T.N. Godavarman case (1996). The 2023 amendment narrows the Act's coverage to only two categories of land: areas officially notified as forests under the Indian Forest Act 1927 or other legislation, and land recorded as forest in government records on or after October 25, 1980. Critics argue this exclusion may allow large areas of forest land to be diverted for non-forest use without requiring central government approval. The Supreme Court issued an interim order in February 2024 directing that the dictionary meaning of "forest" as per the Godavarman judgment should still be followed by states until the matter is fully resolved.

Exemptions for national security and border projects: Strategic linear projects related to national security within 100 kilometres of the International Borders, Line of Actual Control (LAC), and Line of Control (LoC) are exempted from central government approval requirements. Projects of up to 10 hectares for security-related infrastructure and up to 5 hectares in Left Wing Extremism Affected Districts for public utility projects are also exempted. All such exemptions are subject to compensatory afforestation conditions.

Expanded list of permitted forest activities: The amendment expands the list of activities that are not considered "non-forest purposes" and therefore do not require prior central government approval. These new permitted activities include establishment of zoos and safaris owned by the government or any authority in forest areas outside protected areas, ecotourism facilities as per approved working plans, and silvicultural operations for forest regeneration. Supporters say these create livelihood opportunities for forest communities; critics argue these activities may harm forest ecology and wildlife habitats.

The 2023 amendment also affects the rights of tribal and forest dwelling communities. Critics point out that the exclusion of "deemed forests" from the Act's coverage means that such forest land can be diverted without requiring consent from the local Gram Sabha, even though the Forest Rights Act 2006 vests rights over such lands in local forest communities. The amendment is currently being challenged in the Supreme Court, with the constitutional validity of several provisions under examination. In a significant judgment in May 2025, the Supreme Court declared Zudpi jungles as Protected Forests under the Forest Conservation Act, reinforcing that the judicial interpretation of forest conservation laws remains important even as legislative amendments are made.

5.3 Conclusion

In this chapter we have discussed the Forest Conservation Act 1980 and its significant 2023 amendment. The original Act remains one of India's key tools for controlling the diversion of forest land for non-forest purposes, requiring central government approval for such diversions. The 2023 amendment introduces important changes to streamline development approvals, but it also raises questions about the adequacy of forest protection that courts and policymakers continue to address.

Chapter 6: Water Act 1974

In this chapter we discuss the Water Act of 1974, whose objective is to control water pollution and conserve and protect the water bodies of India.

THE WATER (PREVENTION AND CONTROL OF POLLUTION) ACT, 1974

ACT NO. 6 OF 1974

[23rd March, 1974.]

An Act to provide for the prevention and control of water pollution and the maintaining or restoring of wholesomeness of water, for the establishment, with a view to carrying out the purposes aforesaid, of Boards for the prevention and control of water pollution, for conferring on and assigning to such Boards powers and functions relating thereto and for matters connected therewith.

WHEREAS it is expedient to provide for the prevention and control of water pollution and the maintaining or restoring of wholesomeness of water, for the establishment, with a view to carrying out the purposes aforesaid, of Boards for the prevention and control of water pollution and for conferring on and assigning to such Boards powers and functions relating thereto;

AND WHEREAS Parliament has no power to make laws for the States with respect to any of the matters aforesaid except as provided in articles 249 and 250 of the Constitution;

AND WHEREAS in pursuance of clause (1) of article 252 of the Constitution resolutions have been passed by all the Houses of the Legislatures of the States of Assam, Bihar, Gujarat, Haryana, Himachal Pradesh, Jammu and Kashmir, Karnataka, Kerala, Madhya Pradesh, Rajasthan, Tripura and West Bengal to the effect that the matters aforesaid should be regulated in those States by Parliament by law.

BE it enacted by Parliament in the Twenty-fifth Year of the Republic of India as follows:—

CHAPTER I
PRELIMINARY

1. Short title, application and commencement.—(*1*) This Act may be called the Water (Prevention and Control of Pollution) Act, 1974.

(*2*) It applies in the first instance to the whole of the States of Assam, Bihar, Gujarat, Haryana, Himachal Pradesh, Jammu and Kashmir, Karnataka, Kerala, Madhya Pradesh, Rajasthan, Tripura and West Bengal and the Union territories; and it shall apply to such other State which adopts this Act by resolution passed in that behalf under clause (1) of article 252 of the Constitution.

(*3*) It shall come into force, at once in the States of Assam, Bihar, Gujarat, Haryana, Himachal Pradesh, Jammu and Kashmir, Karnataka, Kerala, Madhya Pradesh, Rajasthan, Tripura and West Bengal and in the Union territories, and in any other State which adopts this Act under clause (1) of article 252 of the Constitution on the date of such adoption and any reference in this Act to the commencement of this Act shall, in relation to any State or Union territory, mean the date on which this Act comes into force in such State or Union territory.

2. Definitions.—In this Act, unless the context otherwise requires,—

(*a*) "Board" means the Central Board or a State Board;

[(*b*) "Central Board" means the Central Pollution Control Board constituted under section 3;]

Figure: First page of the Water Act 1974

6.1 Summary of the Water Act

Water pollution is a severe problem all over the world, but especially in India. Waters are polluted due to dumping of sewage, wastes and industrial effluents. Pollution renders waters in rivers and lakes unusable and undrinkable and threatens the health of communities who depend on such water for daily uses. Hence, the Water Prevention and Control of Pollution Act 1974 was brought to prevent water pollution and maintain wholesomeness and purity in the quality of water in natural water bodies all over India.

The definition of pollution as per the water act is as follows:

"pollution" means such contamination of water or such alteration of the physical, chemical or biological properties of water or such discharge of any sewage or trade effluent or of any other liquid, gaseous or solid substance into water (whether directly or indirectly) as may, or is likely to, create a nuisance or render such water harmful or injurious to public health or safety, or to domestic, commercial, industrial, agricultural or other legitimate uses, or to the life and health of animals or plants or of aquatic organisms;

The act provides for establishment of various statutory boards, namely Central Pollution Control Board (CPCB) and State Pollution Control Boards, to control water pollution and various aspects of conservation.

The act regulates the discharge of effluents and pollutants in rivers and lakes, especially from industrial activities such as factories, by providing standards for such effluents and mentioning procedures to be followed for the analysis of samples for inspection. It provides for penalties for non-compliance.

An accompanying act walled the Water (Prevention and Control of Pollution) Cess Act 1977 provides for a cess to entities involved in such industrial activities, which will be used by the pollution control boards to effectively monitor and reduce pollution.

The original act has been amended several times to make it stricter and ensure effective compliance and better enforcement.

6.2 Conclusion

In this chapter we have discussed the water act, which is the main act in India to control water pollution from industrial effluents.

Chapter 7: Air Act 1981

In this chapter we discuss the Air Act 1981, which is the main act in India to control and reduce air pollution. It is similar to the Water Act of 1974 that aims to control water pollution.

Figure: First page of the Air Act 1981

7.1 Summary of the Air Act

Air pollution is caused mainly from human activities such as discharge of industrial wastes into the air and burning of crops and pollution from motor vehicles, power plants and internal combustion engines. Air pollutants include particulate matter, lead, carbon monoxide, sulphur dioxide and other toxic substances

Air pollution is a huge problem in India, rendering the air unbreathable and being responsible for various health problems. The Air (Prevention and Control of Pollution) Act 1981 is an act to control air pollution all over India.

Similar to the Water Act, the Air Act provides for additional inclusion of air pollution control in the various statutory boards at central and state levels for control of pollution, namely Central Pollution Control Board (CPCB) and State Pollution Control Boards. The CPCB enforces the provisions at the central and union territory level and the SPCBs at the levels of various states.

The definitions of air pollution and air pollutant under the air act are as follows:

*(a) "**air pollutant**" means any solid, liquid or gaseous substance [(including noise)] present in the atmosphere in such concentration as may be or tend to be injurious to human beings or other living creatures or plants or property or environment;*

*(b) "**air pollution**" means the presence in the atmosphere of any air pollutant;*

The air act stipulates the constitution and powers of the pollution control boards such as setting standards of emission from automobiles and industrial plants. Emission of air pollution in excess of the standards set is prohibited. The boards can send officials to inspect various industrial plants, equipment used and manufacturing processes and collect samples to be analysed in laboratories, to ensure air quality is as per the standards set. The air act also prescribes penalties for various violations and offences by individuals, companies and even government departments. Under the act, state governments can designate air pollution areas, in which operating industrial plants cannot be done unless prior consent from the state pollution control boards is obtained.

7.2 Conclusion

In this chapter, we have discussed the Air Act of 1981 and its various provisions to control air pollution in India.

Chapter 8: Environment Protection Act 1986

In this chapter we discuss the Environment Protection Act 1986. It is an umbrella act having a range of provisions related to protection of the environment.

THE ENVIRONMENT (PROTECTION) ACT, 1986

No. 29 OF 1986

[23rd May, 1986.]

An Act to provide for the protection and improvement of environment and for matters connected there with;

WHEREAS the decisions were taken at the United Nations Conference on the Human Environment held at Stockholm in June, 1972, in which India participated, to take appropriate steps for the protection and improvement of human environment;

AND WHEREAS it is considered necessary further to implement the decisions aforesaid in so far as they relate to the protection and improvement of environment and the prevention of hazards to human beings, other living creatures, plants and property;

BE it enacted by Parliament in the Thirty-seventh Year of the Republic of India as follows:-

CHAPTER I
PRELIMINARY

1. SHORT TITLE, EXTENT AND COMMENCEMENT.-

(1) This Act may be called the Environment (Protection) Act, 1986.

(2) It extends to the whole of India.

(3) It shall come into force on such date as the Central Government may, by notification in the Official Gazette, appoint and different dates may be appointed for different provisions of this Act and for different areas[1].

2. DEFINITIONS.-

In this Act, unless the context otherwise requires,--

(a) "environment" includes water, air and land and the inter- relationship which exists among and between water, air and land, and human beings, other living creatures, plants, micro-organism and property;

Figure: First page of the Environment Protection Act 1986

8.1 Introduction to the Environment Protection Act 1986

The Environment Protection Act was brought as a response to the Bhopal Gas Tragedy of 1984, where the leak of gases from the Union Carbide pesticide plant in Bhopal killed or injured hundreds of thousands of people and is known as the worst industrial disaster in the history of the world. The act was intended to implement international agreements for protection of the environment signed by India, such as the 1972 UN conference on the environment at Stockholm.

The Environment Protection Act is an umbrella legislation that provides a framework for the environmental regulation regime in India and planning and implementing long-term regulations for environmental safety and response to situations threatening the environment.

8.2 Provisions of the Environment Protection Act 1986

The act lays the following powers of the central government:

(i) Co-ordination of actions by the State Governments, officers and other authorities (a) under this Act, or the rules made thereunder, or (b) under any other law for the time being in force which is relatable to the objects of this Act;

(ii) planning and execution of a nation-wide programme for the prevention, control and abatement of environmental pollution;

(iii) laying down standards for the quality of environment in its various aspects;

(iv) laying down standards for emission or discharge of environmental pollutants from various sources whatsoever: Provided that different standards for emission or discharge may be laid down under this clause from different sources having regard to the quality or composition of the emission or discharge of environmental pollutants from such sources;

(v) restriction of areas in which any industries, operations or processes or class of industries, operations or processes shall not be carried out or shall be carried out subject to certain safeguards;

(vi) laying down procedures and safeguards for the prevention of accidents which may cause environmental pollution and remedial measures for such accidents;

(vii) laying down procedures and safeguards for the handling of hazardous substances;

(viii) examination of such manufacturing processes, materials and substances as are likely to cause environmental pollution;

(ix) carrying out and sponsoring investigations and research relating to problems of environmental pollution;

(x) inspection of any premises, plant, equipment, machinery, manufacturing or other processes, materials or substances and giving, by order, of such directions to such authorities, officers or persons as it may consider necessary to take steps for the prevention, control and abatement of environmental pollution;

(xi) establishment or recognition of environmental laboratories and institutes to carry out the functions entrusted to such environmental laboratories and institutes under this Act;

(xii) collection and dissemination of information in respect of matters relating to environmental pollution;

(xiii) preparation of manuals, codes or guides relating to the prevention, control and abatement of environmental pollution;

(xiv) such other matters as the Central Government deems necessary or expedient for the purpose of securing the effective implementation of the provisions of this Act.

As per the act, the central government has power to make rules to regulate environmental pollution, such as setting standards for air, water and soil quality, and fixing the maximum allowable concentration of emission of pollutants.

The act covers major industrial and infrastructure activities and prohibits and regulates specific activities in coastal areas and eco-sensitive areas, with 10 km buffer zones being set up around such areas. The act also has provisions for regulating the location of industries away from ecologically sensitive areas, management of hazardous wastes, and protection of public health and welfare.

The Act also provides for coordination of the activities of various central and state authorities established under other environment-related laws, such as the Water Act and the Air Act. It has provisions for inspections of plants etc by the authorities. It also provides penalties for non-compliance and environmental offences, including offences by government departments. These penalties include imprisonment up to five years or with fine up to Rs 100000, or both, and worse for repeat offences.

In practice, the act is enforced by the Central Pollution Control Board and the numerous State Pollution Control Boards, entities previously established by the water act and air act. The government also has powers to notify additional rules under the act.

The following statutory bodies have been set up under the act:

- Genetic Engineering Appraisal Committee

- National Coastal Zone Management Authority

8.3 The ozone-depleting substances (regulation and control) rules 2000.

These rules are constituted under the Environment Protection Act. These rules are meant to protect the ozone layer on the earth's atmosphere, that protects us from sun's UV rays which can be harmful for the skin. These rules regulate the production and trade of ozone depleting substances, which damage the ozone layer. Such substances mainly come under the class of chlorofluorocarbons or CFCs and Hydroflorochlorocarbons of HCFCs. CFCs were originally used widely as aerosol propellants, before they were banned under ozone regulations such as this and similar resolutions by other countries. The rules also prohibit the use of other ozone depleting substances including halons, ODSs such as carbon tetrachloride and methyl chloroform, and SFC except in metered-dose inhalers and for other medical purposes.

8.4 Conclusion

In this chapter we have discussed the environment protection act of 1986 and its various provisions.

Chapter 9: Coastal Regulation Zone Notification 2018

In this chapter we discuss the coastal regulation zone notifications, for protection of coastal areas of India.

9.1 Summary of the Coastal Regulation Zone Notifications

The Coastal Regulation Zone Notification rules are intended to protect the fragile ecosystem in coastal zones of India, that are threatened by rapid development and deforestation. The aim is to promote sustainable development in the zones while considering natural hazards such as increasing sea levels due to global warming. They also aim to protect biodiversity in the coastal zones and provide livelihood security to local coastal communities such as fishermen.

The Coastal Regulation Zones have been classified into 4 zones for regulation:

- CRZ I: these include ecologically sensitive areas such as mangroves, coral reefs, salt marshes, turtle nesting ground, and the inter-tidal zone.

- CRZ II: These include areas close to the shoreline, and which have been developed.
- CRZ III: These include coastal areas that are not substantially built up, including rural coastal areas.
- CRZ IV: These include water area from Low Tide Line (LTL) to the limit of territorial waters of India.

As per the notification, development in these zones will need varying level of clearances from the central and state governments. CRZ 1 and 4 need clearance from central government while 2 and 3 need clearance from state governments.

9.2 Conclusion

In this chapter, we have discussed the coastal regulation zone notifications, intended to protect the biodiversity of the coastal zones.

Chapter 10: Hazardous Waste Management Regulations

In this chapter we discuss the hazardous waste management regulations of the government of India. These include the Hazardous Wastes Rules 2008, Biomedical Waste Rules 1998, Municipal Solid Wastes Rules 2000, and Batteries Rules 2001.

10.1 Introduction to hazardous waste management regulations

Hazardous Waste Management Rules are notified to ensure safe handling, generation, processing, treatment, package, storage, transportation, use reprocessing, collection, conversion, and offering for sale, destruction and disposal of Hazardous Waste. If hazardous waste is left unchecked and released into the air or water or soil they can play havoc with the environment. That is why it is important to have a proper system to deal with such waste.

As per the Hazardous wastes management rules 2008, the definition of hazardous wastes is as follows:

Hazardous waste means any waste which, by reason of any of its physical, chemical, reactive, toxic, flammable, explosive or corrosive characteristics, causes danger or is likely to cause danger to health or environment, whether alone or when in contact with other wastes or substances.

The objective of the hazardous waste management rules in India is to enable the government to ensure proper treatment and disposal and environmentally sound management of the hazardous wastes. The rules aim at dealing with the management of solid waste including their segregation at source, transportation of waste, treatment and final disposal.

10.2 The Hazardous Wastes (Management, Handling and Transboundary) Rules 2008

These hazardous waste management rules have guidance for manufacture, storage and import of hazardous chemicals and for management of hazardous wastes. As per the rules, the occupier is responsible for the environmentally sound management of hazardous wastes, they need to ensure that contaminants in the waste that are harmful to the environment are contained and accidents are prevented.

The State Pollution Control Board has to provide an authorization to any individual or entity that is engaged in generation, collection, processing, destruction or conversion of such wastes. They will be collected and recycled, stored and disposed in designated sites that are notified by the State Pollution Control Board. The occupiers shall maintain a record of the storage of such wastes as well and such records can be inspected by the State Pollution Control Board.

The rules also contain procedures for recycling and reuse of hazardous wastes. The central pollution control board or state boards have to give authorization to the entity who wishes to perform this task, after verifying that they comply with the emission standards and standards for treatment of hazardous wastes, use environmentally sound technologies and have the technical capabilities and facilities for recycling of such wastes.

The rules also provides regulations for import and export of such wastes, procedures for storage, labelling and packaging of the wastes while transport, and keep the records that may be inspected by pollution control boards at the central and state levels. The rules also have a list of processes generating hazardous wastes, a list of wastes with their concentration limits, and lists of hazardous characteristic such as flammable and toxic substances.

10.3 Biomedical Waste (Management and Handling) Rules 1998

These rules were formulated similar to those for hazardous waste. They provide the procedure for proper disposal, segregation, and transport of biomedical wastes and the person or entity has to take proper authorization. The biomedical wastes include animal waste, medical equipment such as syringes, biotechnology and microbiology wastes and chemical waste. The prescribed authorities overseeing the procedures are the state and central pollution control boards.

10.4 Municipal Solid Wastes (Management and Handling) Rules 2000

These rules are meant to regulate handling of wastes by the municipal authorities. They enable the municipal authorities to handle and dispose municipal solid waste in an environment friendly manner.

10.5 Batteries (Management & Handling) Rules 2001

These rules deal with the proper and effective management and handling of lead acid batteries waste. The Act requires all entities handling such waste, including manufacturers, assemblers and so on to comply with the provisions of these rules.

10.6 Conclusion

In this chapter we have discussed a few rules related to management of hazardous waste.

Chapter 11: Energy Conservation Act 2001

In this chapter we discuss the energy conservation Act 2001 which is intended to reduce the energy wastage and improve energy efficiency. Since energy is extracted from the environment, the reduced energy wastage is a key factor for environmental conservation as well.

> THE ENERGY CONSERVATION ACT, 2001
>
> ACT No. 52 OF 2001
>
> [29th September, 2001.]
>
> An Act to provide for efficient use of energy and its conservation and for matters connected therewith or incidental thereto.
>
> BE it enacted by Parliament in the Fifty-second Year of the Republic of India as follows:—
>
> CHAPTER I
>
> PRELIMINARY
>
> **1. Short title, extent and commencement.**—(*1*) This Act may be called the Energy Conservation Act, 2001.
>
> (*2*) It extends to the whole of India except the State of Jammu and Kashmir.
>
> (*3*) It shall come into force on such date[1] as the Central Government may, by notification in the Official Gazette, appoint; and different dates may be appointed for different provisions of this Act and any reference in any such provision to the commencement of this Act shall be construed as a reference to the coming into force of that provision.
>
> **2. Definitions.**—In this Act, unless the context otherwise requires,—
>
> (*a*) "accredited energy auditor" means [2][an energy auditor accredited in accordance with the provisions of] clause (*p*) of sub-section (*2*) of section 13;
>
> (*b*) "Appellate Tribunal" means the Appellate Tribunal for Energy Conservation [3][referred to in section 30];
>
> [4][(*c*) "building" means any structure or erection or part of structure or erection after the rules relating to energy conservation building codes have been notified under clause (*p*) of section 14 and clause (*a*) of section 15 and includes any existing structure or erection or part of structure or erection, which is having a connected load of 100 Kilowatt (kW) or contract demand of 120 Kilo-volt Ampere (kVA) and above and is used or intended to be used for commercial purposes;]
>
> (*d*) "Bureau" means the Bureau of Energy Efficiency established under sub-section (*1*) of

Figure: First page of the Energy Conservation Act 2001

11.1 Summary of the energy conservation act 2001

The Energy Conservation Act 2001 promotes energy savings and energy conservation in consumer appliances and buildings.

The energy conservation act 2001 was enacted to improve the energy efficiency and reducing wastage. It specifies the energy consumption standards for equipment and appliances.

As part of the act, a Bureau of Energy Efficiency of BEE is a statutory body constituted by the central government under this act. It comprises of the power minister, secretaries, ex officio members who are leaders of various energy institutes and a director general.

The function of the bureau is to ensure energy efficiency by recommending measures for the same such as notifying labels on appliances, setting energy consumption norms and standards and directing energy consumers to meet with the standards, setting guidelines and building codes for energy conservation in commercial buildings and so on. The central government also has the power to issue energy savings certificates.

11.2 Energy Conservation (Amendment) Act 2022 and Carbon Credit Trading Scheme

A major amendment to the Energy Conservation Act 2001 was passed by the Indian Parliament in December 2022 and came into force on January 1, 2023. This amendment, known as the Energy Conservation (Amendment) Act 2022, introduced significant new provisions to align India's energy and climate policy with its international commitments under the Paris Agreement.

India, as a signatory to the Paris Agreement of 2015, committed to reduce the greenhouse gas emission intensity of its economy by 45% by 2030 compared to 2005 levels, and to achieve net-zero carbon emissions by 2070. The Energy Conservation (Amendment) Act 2022 was a key legislative step toward fulfilling these goals. The key new provisions of the amendment include the following:

Carbon Credit Trading Scheme (CCTS): The amendment empowers the central government to specify a Carbon Credit Trading Scheme. A carbon credit is a tradeable permit allowing the holder to emit a specified amount of greenhouse gases. The scheme, formally notified in June 2023, established the Indian Carbon Market (ICM). Under the scheme, large industrial entities in nine obligated sectors — including cement, aluminium, steel, fertiliser, pulp and paper, petroleum refinery, petrochemicals, chlor-alkali, and textiles — are assigned greenhouse gas emission intensity targets. Companies that reduce emissions below their targets earn Carbon Credit Certificates (CCCs), each representing one tonne of CO2 equivalent, which they can sell to other entities. This market-based mechanism is designed to drive decarbonisation of Indian industry. The Carbon Credit Trading Scheme replaced the earlier Perform, Achieve and Trade (PAT) scheme that had focused on energy efficiency.

Obligation to use non-fossil energy sources: The amendment empowers the central government to mandate that designated large industrial consumers must meet a specified minimum share of their energy needs from non-fossil sources such as solar, wind or other renewables. This provision is intended to accelerate India's transition toward clean energy.

Energy Conservation Building Codes: The amendment extended the applicability of energy conservation building codes to large residential and office buildings with a connected load of 100 kilowatts or more, in addition to commercial buildings already covered.

The Indian Carbon Market is structured with multiple regulatory bodies working together. The Bureau of Energy Efficiency (BEE) acts as the market administrator and issues Carbon Credit Certificates. The Grid Controller of India maintains the central registry recording all transactions. The Central Electricity Regulatory Commission (CERC) regulates trading to ensure fairness. Independent Accredited Carbon Verification Agencies verify the emission reduction data of participating companies. A National Steering

Committee for the Indian Carbon Market (NSCICM) provides policy direction. Registration under the CCTS began from January 2025, and the scheme is expected to be fully operational by 2026. In March 2025, the government approved eight methodologies for implementing the scheme, including renewable energy, green hydrogen production, industrial energy efficiency, landfill methane recovery, and mangrove afforestation and reforestation.

The CCTS is also relevant to international trade. Under the European Union's Carbon Border Adjustment Mechanism (CBAM), which taxes carbon-intensive imports, Indian companies with verified CCTS credits may use those credits to offset CBAM charges, facilitating smoother access to European markets.

11.3 Conclusion

In this chapter, we have discussed the Energy Conservation Act 2001 and its 2022 amendment. Together, these acts form the legal backbone of India's efforts to promote energy efficiency, reduce dependence on fossil fuels, and build a market-based framework for carbon emission trading, which are all crucial elements of India's commitment to addressing climate change.

Chapter 12: Scheduled Tribes and Other Traditional Forest Dwellers (Recognition of Forest Rights) Act, 2006 (FRA)

In this chapter, we discuss the Scheduled Tribes and Other Traditional Forest Dwellers Act 2006, also called the Forest Rights Act. This act recognizes the unique rights of forest dwelling scheduled tribes to use the forest resources.

12.1 Summary of the Forest Rights Act

Tribal communities have been dwelling in Indian forests for thousands of years. They follow traditional lifestyles and livelihoods. Before this act came into being, their unique lifestyles and rights to the forest resources were not recognized, consequently they were often evicted or oppressed by various unscrupulous agents. The forest rights act seeks to remedy the same.

The Forest Rights act empowers the forest dwelling communities to continue to use the forest resources as they were used traditionally, and protects them from unlawful evictions. It recognizes and vests the forest rights and occupation in forest land in Forest Dwelling Scheduled Tribes and others residing in such forests for generations.

PUBLISHED BY AUTHORITY

सं. 2 नई दिल्ली, मंगलवार, जनवरी 2, 2007/ पौष 12, 1928
No. 2 NEW DELHI, TUESDAY, JANUARY 2, 2007/PAUSA 12, 1928

इस भाग में भिन्न पृष्ठ संख्या दी जाती है जिससे कि यह अलग संकलन के रूप में रखा जा सके।
Separate paging is given to this Part in order that it may be filed as a separate compilation

MINISTRY OF LAW AND JUSTICE
(Legislative Department)

New Delhi, the 2nd January, 2007/Pausa 12, 1928 (Saka)

The following Act of Parliament received the assent of the President on the 29th December, 2006, and is hereby published for general information:-

THE SCHEDULED TRIBES AND OTHER TRADITIONAL FOREST DWELLERS (RECOGNITION OF FOREST RIGHTS) ACT, 2006

No. 2 of 2007

[29th December, 2006]

An Act to recognize and vest the forest rights and occupation in forest land in forest dwelling Scheduled Tribes and other traditional forest dwellers who have been residing in such forests for generations but whose rights could not be recorded; to provide for a framework for recording the forest rights so vested and the nature of evidence required for such recognition and vesting in respect of forest land.

WHEREAS the recognised rights of the forest dwelling Scheduled Tribes and other traditional forest dwellers include the responsibilities and authority for sustainable use, conservation of biodiversity and maintenance of ecological balance and thereby strengthening the conservation regime of the forests while ensuring livelihood and food security of the forest dwellings Scheduled Tribes and other traditional forest dwellers;

AND WHEREAS the forest rights on ancestral lands and their habitat were not adequately recognised in the consolidation of State forests during the colonial period as well as in independent India resulting in historical injustice to the forest dwelling Scheduled Tribes and other traditional forest dwellers who are integral to the very survival and sustainability of the forest ecosystem;

AND WHEREAS it has become necessary to address the long standing insecurity of tenurial and access rights of forest dwelling Scheduled Tribes and other traditional forest dwellers including those who were forced to relocate their dwelling due to State development interventions.

BE it enacted by Parliament in the Fifty-seventh Year of the Republic of India as follows:-

Figure: First page of the Forest Rights Act 2006

The objectives of the act are as follows:

- To undo the historical injustices to the forest dwelling communities

- To ensure land tenure, livelihood and food security of the forest dwelling Scheduled Tribes and other traditional forest dwellers
- To strengthen the conservation regime of the forests by including the responsibilities and authority on Forest Rights holders for sustainable use, conservation of biodiversity and maintenance of ecological balance.

This act comes under the Ministry of Tribal Affairs.

The act establishes the responsibilities and authority for sustainable use, conservation of biodiversity, and maintenance of the ecological balance of the forests, as well as ensure the livelihood and food of the forest dwellers.

The act identifies four types of rights of the forest dwellers:

- Rights to hold and live in forest land. This includes the rights to ownership of land farmed by tribals or forest dwellers.
- Community rights to forest dwellers including fish and aquatic resources and grazing and pasture. These include rights to extract minor forest produce.
- Right to rehabilitation in case of illegal eviction or forced displacement.

- Right to protect, regenerate or conserve or manage any community forest resources that are traditionally being used.

The process for approval of these rights is via a proposal from the gram sabha of the local village or forest area, after which it passes through two levels of screening at the taluka and district levels before approval.

12.2 Conclusion

In this chapter we have discussed the forest rights act, that seeks to preserve the rights of traditional forest communities on forest land.

Chapter 13: Biological Diversity Act 2002

In this chapter we discuss the biological diversity act 2002. It is an act aimed to preserve the biological diversity in India and the sharing of benefits from biological resources.

THE BIOLOGICAL DIVERSITY ACT, 2002

ACT No. 18 OF 2003

[5th February, 2003.]

An Act to provide for conservation of biological diversity, sustainable use of its components and fair and equitable sharing of the benefits arising out of the use of biological resources, knowledge and for matters connected therewith or incidental thereto.

WHEREAS India is rich in biological diversity and associated traditional and contemporary knowledge system relating thereto.

AND WHEREAS India is a party to the United Nations Convention on Biological Diversity signed at Rio de Janeiro on the 5th day of June, 1992;

AND WHEREAS the said Convention came into force on the 29th December, 1993;

AND WHEREAS the said Convention reaffirms the sovereign rights of the States over their biological resources;

AND WHEREAS the said Convention has the main objective of conservation of biological diversity, sustainable use of its components and fair and equitable sharing of the benefits arising out of utilisation of genetic resources;

AND WHEREAS it is considered necessary to provide for conservation, sustainable utilisation and equitable sharing of the benefits arising out of utilisation of genetic resources and also to give effect to the said Convention.

BE it enacted by Parliament in the Fifty-third Year of the Republic of India as follows:—

CHAPTER I

PRELIMINARY

1. Short title, extent and commencement.—(*1*) This Act may be called the Biological Diversity Act, 2002.

(*2*) It extends to the whole of India.

(*3*) It shall come into force on such date[1] as the Central Government may, by notification in the Official Gazette, appoint:

Provided that different dates may be appointed for different provisions of this Act and any reference in any such provision to the commencement of this Act shall be construed as a reference to the coming

Figure: First page of the Biological Diversity Act 2002

13.1 Introduction to the Biological Diversity Act 2002

The Biological Diversity Act 2002 aims to preserve the biological diversity of India and check biopiracy, such as foreign companies patenting traditional biological resources or remedies. It was inspired by the United Nations Convention on Biological Diversity (CBD) 1992 in which India too participated and which recognizes the rights of countries to their own biological resources.

The act has the following definition of biological diversity:

"biological diversity" means the variability among living organisms from all sources and the ecological complexes of which they are part and includes diversity within species or between species and of eco-systems;

The act sets up the following bodies:

- National Biodiversity Authority
- State Biodiversity Boards
- Biodiversity Management Committees

The act holds that biodiversity related activities cannot be undertaken without the approval of the National Biodiversity Authority. Any person or organization must apply to the authority before applying for a patent or intellectual property protection in this area. The authority is to advise the central government on matters of biodiversity, sustainable use of its components and equitable sharing of benefits out of usage of biological resources.

The goals of this act include protection of traditional knowledge, prevention of biopiracy, and prohibition of people and companies from applying for patents without government permission.

The act also has provisions for the development of national and state plans for the conservation of biodiversity, state notification and conservation of biological diversity areas, and notification of endangered species. It also seeks to ensure that benefits from available biological resources, their by-products, knowledge and related practices are equitably shared between the person or organization applying for acquiring such benefits (such as patents) and the local bodies involved.

13.2 Biological Diversity (Amendment) Act 2023 and Biodiversity Rules 2024

Two major updates to India's biodiversity legal framework came in 2023 and 2024. The Biological Diversity (Amendment) Act 2023 was passed by Parliament in 2023 and came into force on April 1, 2024. This amendment introduced the following key changes:

Decriminalisation: All violations under the original Biological Diversity Act 2002 that previously attracted criminal penalties were decriminalised. Offences are now addressed through civil penalties rather than criminal prosecution.

Exemptions for AYUSH and local communities: Registered AYUSH practitioners, local communities, biodiversity growers, and cultivators are now exempted from the requirement of notifying the State Biodiversity Boards before using biological resources for commercial purposes, provided this use is in accordance with traditional practices. This exemption was intended to promote the traditional Indian systems of medicine such as Ayurveda, Siddha, Unani, and Yoga.

Streamlined patent and research approvals: The amendment seeks to speed up research and patent application processes involving biological resources, aiming to reduce bureaucratic delays that had affected Indian researchers and companies.

Following the 2023 amendment, the Ministry of Environment, Forest and Climate Change notified the Biological Diversity Rules 2024 in October 2024, which came into effect from December 25, 2024, superseding the earlier Biodiversity Rules 2004. The new rules enhance the powers of the National Biodiversity Authority (NBA) and introduce a modern enforcement mechanism including appointment of adjudicating officers for determining penalties. Prior approval from the NBA is now required before the grant of any Intellectual Property Rights over biological resources. The rules also prescribe detailed procedures for access to biological resources and equitable sharing of benefits arising from their use. These changes bring India's biodiversity regulatory framework in closer alignment with the Kunming-Montreal Global Biodiversity Framework adopted at the Convention on Biological Diversity Conference of the Parties (COP-15) in Montreal in December 2022, which sets a global target of protecting 30% of land and water areas by 2030.

13.3 Conclusion

In this chapter we have discussed the Biological Diversity Act 2002 and its subsequent amendments, including the Biological Diversity (Amendment) Act 2023 and the Biodiversity Rules 2024. These laws collectively form India's framework for preserving its rich biodiversity, preventing biopiracy, and ensuring that benefits from biological resources are equitably shared with local communities. The ongoing evolution of these rules reflects the need to balance conservation objectives with the promotion of traditional knowledge systems and scientific research.

Chapter 14: National Green Tribunal Act (NGT) 2010

In this chapter we discuss the National Green Tribunal Act 2010. The main purpose of this act was the setting up of the National Green Tribunal, which is a special tribunal to speedily handle cases related to environmental issues. The setting up of the tribunal has given teeth to the various environmental acts in India.

14.1 Introduction to the National Green Tribunal Act 2010

The National Green Tribunal Act 2010 was established to provide remedies for pollution and environmental damages and thus to conserve the environment in a more effective way. The National Green Tribunal (NGT) was established in 2010 by the government of India. It is a specialised body dedicated to speedily deciding cases related to environmental protection. It thus aims to reduce the burden on higher courts in environment related cases.

The idea was to keep pollution, especially caused by industrial effluents, to within manageable levels and thus ensure sustainable development, which is especially important for a rapidly developing country like India. For this, it is important to ensure speedy remedies and compensation to victims of pollution and environmental damage.

EXTRAORDINARY

भाग II — खण्ड 1

PART II — Section 1

प्राधिकार से प्रकाशित

PUBLISHED BY AUTHORITY

सं॰ 25]	नई दिल्ली, बुधवार, जून 2, 2010 / ज्येष्ठ 12, 1932
No. 25]	NEW DELHI, WEDNESDAY, JUNE 2, 2010 / JYAISTHA 12, 1932

इस भाग में भिन्न पृष्ठ संख्या दी जाती है जिससे कि यह अलग संकलन के रूप में रखा जा सके।
Separate paging is given to this Part in order that it may be filed as a separate compilation.

MINISTRY OF LAW AND JUSTICE

(Legislative Department)

New Delhi, the 2nd June, 2010/Jyaistha 12, 1932 (Saka)

The following Act of Parliament received the assent of the President on the 2nd June, 2010, and is hereby published for general information:—

THE NATIONAL GREEN TRIBUNAL ACT, 2010

(No. 19 OF 2010)

[2nd June, 2010.]

An Act to provide for the establishment of a National Green Tribunal for the effective and expeditious disposal of cases relating to environmental protection and conservation of forests and other natural resources including enforcement of any legal right relating to environment and giving relief and compensation for damages to persons and property and for matters connected therewith or incidental thereto.

AND WHEREAS India is a party to the decisions taken at the United Nations Conference on the Human Environment held at Stockholm in June, 1972, in which India participated, calling upon the States to take appropriate steps for the protection and improvement of the human environment;

AND WHEREAS decisions were taken at the United Nations Conference on Environment and Development held at *Rio de Janeiro* in June, 1992, in which India participated, calling upon the States to provide effective access to judicial and administrative proceedings, including redress and remedy and to develop national laws regarding liability and compensation for the victims of pollution and other environmental damage;

Figure: Front page of the National Green Tribunal Act 2010

The act defines its own purpose as follows:

An Act to provide for the establishment of a National Green Tribunal for the effective and expeditious disposal of cases relating to environmental protection and conservation of forests and other natural resources including enforcement of any legal right relating to environment and giving relief and compensation for damages to persons and property and for matters connected therewith or incidental thereto.

14.2 National Green Tribunal under the Act

The National Green tribunal was set up under this act as a response of Indian government to the Rio Summit or the United Nations Conference on Environment and Development in Rio de Janeiro in Brazil in 1992, which was an international summit bringing together all countries to take urgent coordinated action on environmental issues lest the survival of humanity be threatened by environmental damage. An earlier UN conference related to the environment in Stockholm in 1972, where India also participated, was also mentioned as inspiration for the act. Another inspiration mentioned is Article 21 of the Constitution, which gives the right of citizens to a healthy environment.

The National Green Tribunal, which was constituted under this act, has five branches with regional jurisdictions in New Delhi (North), Pune (West), Bhopal (Central), Chennai (South) and Kolkata (East).

The tribunal comprises the following members, who have terms of five years in the tribunal:

- A full-time chairperson. The chairperson of the tribunal is usually a retired judge of the Supreme court.
- 10 to 20 judicial members, which usually comprise other retired judges of high courts
- 10 to 20 expert members in the field of environmental conservation. These must have administrative experience of at least 15 years, 5 of which must be in the field of environmental conservation.

The tribunal has jurisdiction over civil cases that are related mainly to the environment, such as damage caused to the environment or from pollution, protection of forests and other natural resources and enforcement of environmental legal claims. The remedies it gives can include the following:

- Relief and compensation to victims of pollution and environmental damage, including instances of death, injury or damage

- Restitution of property damaged
- Restitution of the environment

The National Green Tribunal must resolve environmental cases brought to it within six months, thus ensuring speedy justice.

The tribunal also has appellate jurisdiction for any decision previously made under the following acts:

- Water (Prevention and Control of Pollution) Act 1974
- Water (Prevention and Control Of Pollution) Cess Act 1977
- Air (Prevention and Control of Pollution) Act 1981
- Forest (Conservation) Act 1980
- Environment Protection Act 1986
- Biological Diversity Act 2002
- Forest Conservation Act, 1980
- Public Liability Insurance Act 1991

However, the following two acts have been kept outside its jurisdiction:

- Wildlife Protection Act, 1972

- Scheduled Tribes and Other Traditional Forest Dwellers (Recognition of Forest Rights) Act, 2006 (FRA)

The tribunal can also institute penalties to offending parties in case of non-compliance of its orders.

The appeals against the decisions of the tribunal can be made in the high courts and supreme court.

14.3 Conclusion

In this chapter we have discussed the National Green Tribunal Act and the functions and powers of the National Green Tribunal.

Chapter 15: Wildlife Protection Act 1972

In this chapter we discuss the Wildlife Protection Act 1972, which seeks to protect the plants and animal species of India. It gives a series of species who are protected, with varying degrees of protection for different species based on how much they are important and endangered. It also establishes a few agencies responsible for different crucial aspects of protection of wildlife.

15.1 Summary of Wildlife Protection Act

After decades of poaching and smuggling and encroaching into forests, wildlife in India has become threatened. Several species such as the royal Bengal tiger are endangered. Illegal poaching of tigers and leopards for their skin and elephants for ivory are just some examples.

To prevent such incidents and protect the wildlife of India, the Wildlife Protection Act was enacted in 1972 by the Indian parliament. It imposes restrictions on hunting and poaching and illegal trade in wildlife, provides protection for certain species of wildlife. It establishes protected areas for wildlife such as sanctuaries, national parks and protected reserves. It establishes bodies to manage various zoos, national parks and reserves. It also constitutes a national board for wildlife comprising the prime minister, various ministers and secretaries, as well as state boards.

The original act has been amended several times to make it more effective, especially with the 2002 Amendment Act which made the punishments more stringent and provides for improved enforcement.

THE WILD LIFE (PROTECTION) ACT, 1972

ACT No. 53 OF 1972

[9th September, 1972.]

[An Act to provide for the protection of wild animals, birds and plants and for matters connected therewith or ancillary or incidental thereto with a view to ensuring the ecological and environmental security of the country.]

*

CHAPTER I

PRELIMINARY

1. Short title, extent and commencement.—(*1*) This Act may be called the Wild Life (Protection) Act, 1972.

[(*2*) It extends to the whole of India except the State of Jammu and Kashmir.]

(*3*) It shall come into force in a State or Union territory to which it extends [***] on such date as the Central Government may, by notification, appoint, and different dates may be appointed for different provisions of this Act or for different States or Union territories.

2. Definitions.—In this Act, unless the context otherwise requires,—

[(*1*) "animal" includes amphibians, birds, mammals and reptiles and their young, and also includes, in the cases of birds and reptiles, their eggs;]

(*2*) "animal article" means an article made from any captive animal or wild animal, other than vermin, and includes an article or object in which the whole or any part of such animal [has been used, and ivory imported into India and an article made therefrom];

*

[(*4*) "Board" means a State Board for Wild Life constituted under sub-section (1) of section 6;]

(*5*) "captive animal" means any animal, specified in Schedule I, Schedule II, Schedule III or Schedule IV, which is captured or kept or bred in captivity;

*

(*7*) "Chief Wild Life Warden" means the person appointed as such under clause (*a*) of sub-section (*1*) of section 4;

[(*7A*) "circus" means an establishment, whether stationary or mobile, where animals are kept or used wholly or mainly for the purpose of performing tricks or manoeuvres;]

*

[(*9*) "Collector" means the chief officer in charge of the revenue administration of a district or any other officer not below the rank of a Deputy Collector as may be appointed by the State Government under section 18B in this behalf;]

(*10*) "commencement of this Act", in relation to—

Figure: Front page of the wildlife protection Act 1972

The Wildlife Protection Act provides for the protection of Indian wildlife including endangered animals and plants and also birds, whose species are mentioned in lists. It extends to the whole of India.

15.2 Schedules of the Wildlife Protection Act

The act has six schedules which protect wildlife in varying degrees as follows:

- Schedules 1 and 2 contain a list of species of animals who are given the highest level of protection and offences under these have the highest penalties. The prescribed imprisonment for offences is 3 years to 7 years along with a fine of minimum Rs 10000 with 25000 for subsequent offences. Schedule 1 includes species such as cheetah, blackbuck, tiger and Indian lion, as well as protected amphibians and reptiles such as crocodiles and pythons.

- Schedule 3 and 4 have lists of wildlife species which are also protected, however the penalties are lower than schedule 1 and 2.

- Schedule 5 contains a list of pests or vermin which include common crows, fruit bats, rats and mice which can be freely hunted.

- Schedule 6 contains a list of endemic plants that are prohibited from cultivation and planting. Such plants include pitcher plant and blue and red vanda.

15.3 Statutory bodies set up under the wildlife protection Act

The Wildlife protection act also sets up a number of important statutory bodies whose responsibility lies in different aspects of wildlife protection.

These bodies are as follows:

- National Board for Wildlife and state wildlife advisory boards
- Central Zoo Authority
- Wildlife Crime Control Bureau
- National Tiger Conservation Authority

15.4 Conclusion

In this chapter we have gone through the wildlife protection act and its provisions.

Chapter 16: Conclusion

In this book we have presented an introduction to ecology and environment and gone through a few important laws in India that aim to preserve different aspects of the environment.

India has sufficient laws related to environmental protection, however the challenge is to ensure that they are enforced properly. Different agencies of the government, media, and even common citizens have a responsibility to work jointly towards the goal of environmental preservation.

Since the environment of the world is shared by all the people of different countries, environmental protection cannot be effective if one country alone makes efforts towards it. Global warming and pollution are indeed threatening our very existence. Hence, India and other countries together have to make a concerted effort to cut down on pollution and restore our environment to a pristine state. This is necessary to ensure the survival of this world for the sake of our future generations.

In recent years, India's environmental law landscape has seen significant changes. Several major laws were amended between 2022 and 2025, reflecting the tension between rapid economic development and the imperative of environmental protection. Key developments include the following:

Judicial recognition of the right to a clean environment: In a landmark judgment in April 2024, the Supreme Court of India in M.K. Ranjitsinh vs. Union of India recognised the right to a clean environment free from the adverse effects of climate change as a fundamental right under the Indian Constitution. This is a significant development, reinforcing the link between human rights and environmental protection.

Decriminalisation of environmental offences: Under the Water Act 1974 and the Air Act 1981, rules for imposition of penalty were amended in 2024, decriminalising certain violations by replacing the threat of imprisonment with monetary penalties. Similarly, the Water (Prevention and Control of Pollution) Amendment Act 2024 was issued for certain states and union territories. White category industries, which are the least polluting, were also exempted from certain consent requirements. These changes are intended to ease the compliance burden on businesses while maintaining overall environmental standards.

Climate change commitments: India has committed to a set of climate goals called the "Panchamrit" targets under the Paris Agreement: achieving 500 GW of non-fossil fuel energy capacity by 2030, meeting 50% of energy needs from renewables by 2030, reducing carbon emission intensity by 45% by 2030 compared to 2005, creating an additional carbon sink of 2.5 to 3 billion tonnes of CO2 equivalent through additional forest cover by 2030, and achieving net-zero carbon emissions by 2070. India's Carbon Credit Trading Scheme (CCTS) and Energy Conservation Amendment Act 2022 are domestic legislative tools supporting these targets.

Air quality monitoring and enforcement: Air pollution in the National Capital Region (NCR) continues to be a major public health concern. The Supreme Court has been actively monitoring the situation and in December 2024 took suo moto cognisance of hazardous air pollution in the NCR. New Environment Protection (Manner of Holding Inquiry and Imposition of Penalty) Rules 2024 have been notified to streamline the process of filing complaints and conducting adjudication under the Environment Protection Act 1986.

Looking ahead, India's environmental journey will continue to be shaped by the dual imperatives of development and conservation. Rapid urbanisation, industrialisation, and the need for infrastructure pose constant challenges to forest, water, and air quality. At the same time, growing public awareness, judicial activism, and India's international commitments under the Paris Agreement and the Convention on Biological Diversity provide strong motivation to maintain and improve environmental standards. The effectiveness of India's environmental laws ultimately depends not only on their quality and comprehensiveness but on diligent enforcement, citizen participation, and the willingness of all stakeholders to treat the environment as a shared resource to be protected for future generations.

About the author

Siva Prasad Bose is a retired electrical engineer and writer of introductory guides on aspects of law in India. He is retired after many years of service in Uttar Pradesh Power Corporation Limited (UPPCL, formerly UPSEB). He received his engineering degree from Jadavpur University, Kolkata and has a law degree from Meerut University, Meerut and a BSc from MMH College Ghaziabad. His interests lie in the fields of family law, civil law, law of contracts, and any areas of law related to electric power related issues.

Other books by Siva Prasad Bose

Introduction to Wills and Probate

Senior Citizens Abuse in India: And what to do about it

Introduction to Negotiable Instruments: As per Indian laws

Introduction to Marriage Laws in India

Managing Court Cases with Mental Strength

Self-Publish Books and E-Books in India

Delays in Court Cases in India

Introduction to Patents and Patent Law in India

Introduction to Property Law in India

Introduction to Tort Law in India

www.ingramcontent.com/pod-product-compliance
Lightning Source LLC
Chambersburg PA
CBHW070257220526
45465CB00004B/1642